BEN RICCIO

PIZZA FROM NAPLES

BEN RICCIO

PIZZA FROM NAPLES

NEW
HOLLAND

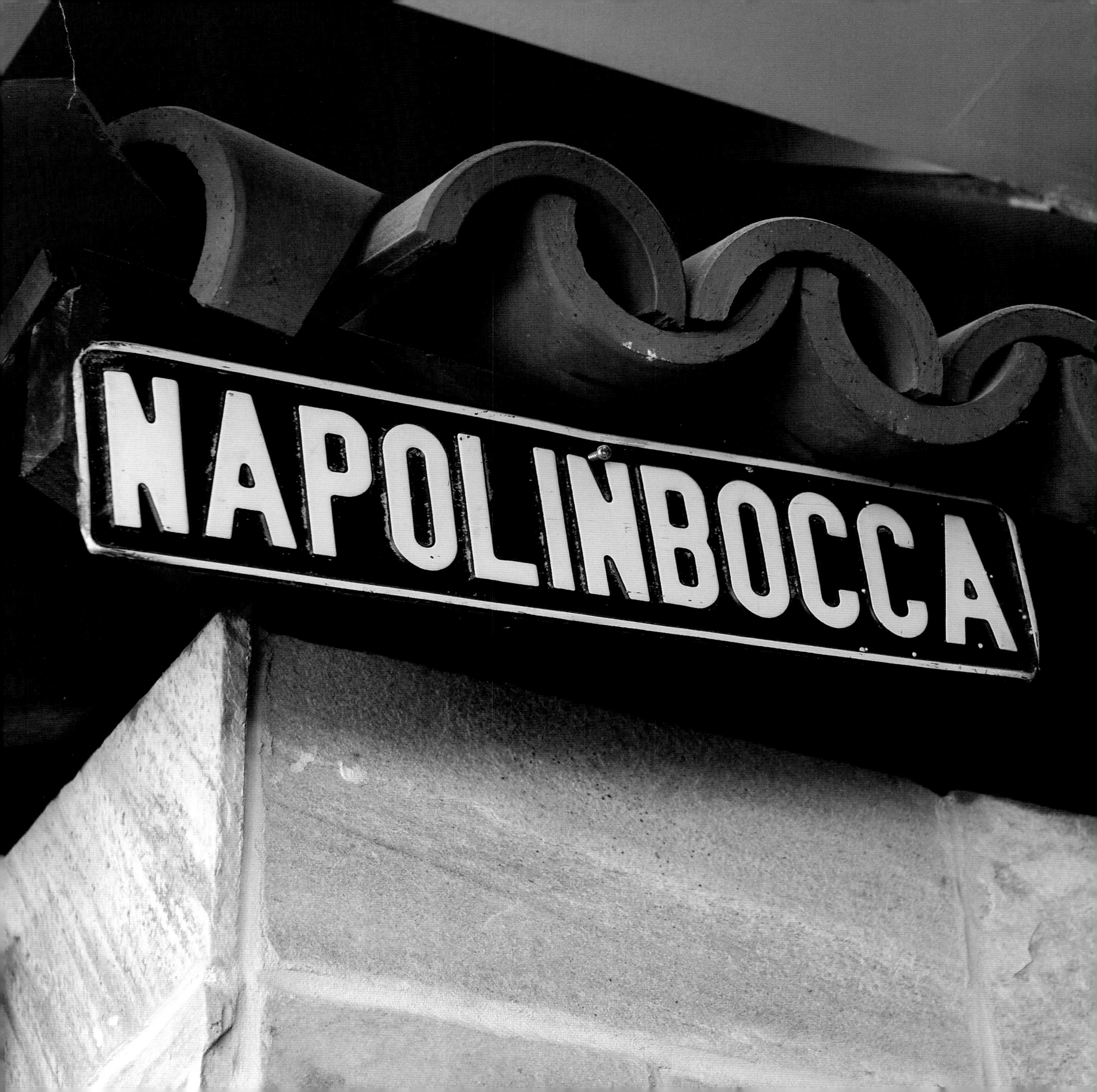
NAPOLINBOCCA

L'ignorante
parla a vanvera,
l'intelligente
parla al momento
opportuno,
il saggio
parla se interpellato,
il fesso
parla sempre.

ACKNOWLEDGEMENTS

I would like to thank God for giving me the strength to make this book. It gives me great pleasure to bring you *Pizza from Naples*. First of all, I'd like to thank my wife, Paula, for supporting me. Then my children, who help me so much in the restaurant and helped Napoli in Bocca become one of the top pizza restaurants in Australia. Special thanks to my good old friend Percy Arena who encouraged me and helped me to put together this book. Finally, thank you to all my patrons who supported me throughout all these years.

CONTENTS

RACCOLTA
DELLI
VENDITORI DI
NAPOLI

INTRODUCTION: PIZZA NAPOLETANA

Even though the pizza was first made by the early Romans, it was the Neapolitan sailors who perfected it in later years.

The Neapolitans were the first to use the tomato, which had arrived in Europe from the New World—America. They readily adapted the tomato, which they found to be full of flavour and with many uses.

However, the now famous use for tomato—as a sauce base for pizza—had not yet been found.

At the time, the poor man's food consisted largely of bread, garlic, oil and herbs, which were readily available, grown locally and cost little to buy or produce.

It was sailors who began to spread tomatoes over the bread crust, their staple food on the boats, to give it more flavour, together with herbs, olive oil and garlic. On returning to Naples, the sailors introduced their new found culinary experience, which soon became very popular with the general public. Thus the origins of the first Pizza came from the Neapolitan sailors.

The bakers, sensing the potential popularity of this new easy-to-make and easy-to-eat meal, began to make a bread crust with tomato and herbs. It became so popular that they named it Pizza Marinara in honor of the sailors (marinari) who first made it on board their ships. Although 'Marinara' means from the sea, the pizza did not contain seafood.

In 1734, the first official Marinara Pizza was made by Da Michelle Pizzeria in Naples. To this day Da Michelle Pizzeria still makes only Pizza Marinara and Pizza Margherita, which was added 155 years later.

The first Pizza Margherita was produced in 1889 by Don Raffaele Esposito at the request of the King of Italy who invited Don Raffaele to the palace to cook for him. To impress the royal family, Raffaele decided to add mozzarella and basil to the traditional tomato pizza. Thus, his pizza displayed the three national colours of Italy: red (tomato), white (mozzarella) and green (basil).

The king was well pleased with the pizza, prompting Don Raffaele to name it 'Pizza Margherita' in honor of Queen Margherita. Don Raffaele's pizza restaurant, Pizzeria Brandi, located in a small lane in Naples, is still visited by tourists today.

In the summer of 2009 I, with my great passion for pizza, visited Pizzeria Brandi and enjoyed a traditional Pizza Margherita, as I stood surrounded by visitors from many countries.

The humble pizza, born from the poor streets of Naples has become a world symbol. From our first traditional Marinara and Margherita, to the seafood, ham and pineapple pizzas we know today, pizza is now enjoyed in every part of the globe.

My restaurant, *Napoli In Bocca,* opened with two family members, me and my wife Paola, and has now grown to seven family members with my children Sonia, Lorenzo and Marco, and their partners Robert and Lisa.With the business being well patronised we began to receive positive reviews from food critics and gained many awards for our traditional pizza restaurant.

In 2006 I decided to refurbish and enlarge *Napoli In Bocca* to accommodate the increasing number of clients who wanted to taste and enjoy traditional Neapolitan cooking and pizza.

Although our pizza is very close to traditional Pizza Napoletana, we are unable to capture that distinct flavour and taste of Naples completely as the ingredients available to us in Australia, such as cheese, are very different to those used in Naples. For example, we use local mozzarella cheese in most of our pizzas but do make a special pizza using Italian Buffalo mozzarella.

We have, however, been able to reproduce the famous 'cornicione' (crust) and thin dough. The thinness of the dough in the centre gives a floppy pizza feel rather than a hard biscuit feel. This floppy base allows the pizza to be folded when eating, in the traditional style, to get the full flavour of the fresh ingredients and our Napoletana sauce.

It makes me feel so proud when clients who have recently returned from Naples tell me that *Napoli In Bocca* reminds them of being in a pizzeria in Naples where the Pizza Margherita tasted very similar, in a room full of people eating and talking loudly.

Napoli In Bocca is run by my family for everyone from young families with children through to their grandparents (*nonni*). Here, they eat and talk just like they do in their home kitchens.

I welcome you and hope you enjoy a Pizza Napoletana with my family.

THE BASICS OF PIZZA MAKING

The basics do not vary, only the ingredients alter for the individual pizza. You need quality dough and fresh ingredients to make a good pizza. All pizza ingredients can be found in supermarkets and delicatessens.

Although it is not difficult to make a pizza at home, it does take a little time to arrive at the finished product, due to the resting and rising process required in preparing the dough. Alternatively, you can use commercially prepared pizza bases, but cooking time may vary, so check with the packet directions before cooking.

Pre-prepared bases are convenient, but the beautifully cooked pizza you will achieve from homemade dough is worth all the time and love you put into the making.

PIZZA DOUGH

This basic dough makes enough for six 30cm (12 inch pizzas). You can roll out the pizza bases, then wrap them in plastic and freeze them for up to 2 months.

30g (1oz) fresh yeast
2 teaspoons salt
600ml (19fl oz) water
1kg (2lb) flour

Into a bowl place fresh yeast and salt in water and mix thoroughly to ensure yeast is fully dissolved.

Place flour in bowl, make a hole in middle and pour in the mixture of water, salt and yeast. Mix all together to form smooth dough.

When smooth, cover with tea towel and leave to rest for at least 1 hour. The dough should rise during this resting time. Make sure the dough has risen to about double its size before cutting or breaking it into pieces.

After the dough has risen, cut or break it into pieces to make six dough balls. The balls can be rolled in the palm of your hands or on the kitchen bench.

Leave the dough balls to rise again for at least 1 hour. The dough can now be stretched with your hands or a rolling pin if you prefer.

TOMATO (NAPOLETANA) SAUCE

4 peeled Roma tomatoes, crushed by hand.
(Alternatively, you can use 1 can of good quality tomatoes)
Extra virgin olive oil
Salt to taste
Garlic
Oregano (if you wish)

Combine all ingredients in a bowl and mix well. Try to prepare sauce a day before and refrigerate to allow ingredients to amalgamate. Extra virgin olive oil is of the highest quality and purity; but you can use regular olive oil if extra virgin olive oil is not available.

It's simple to make a good quality tomato sauce; alternatively there are a number of good bottled sauces readily available in supermarkets.

When pouring tomato sauce over dough, leave at least 1cm ($\frac{1}{2}$ inch) from the edge. This allows the crust around the edge to rise and produce the traditional Pizza Napoletana 'cornicione' (crust). If sauce is poured to the edge of the dough, it will overflow resulting in a messy oven and excess smoke.

Make sure you pour plenty of sauce on the base so that the pizza has that traditional Napoletana sauce taste.

Break dough into pieces, then roll the pieces in the palm of your hands or on the kitchen bench to form balls. Leave the balls to rise for about an hour.

Stretch the dough with your hands or a rolling pin until it is about 2mm ($^1/_{16}$ inch) thick.

The thin dough allows the pizza base to become floppy, like traditional Napoletana pizza.

CHEESE

High-fat mozzarella is preferable as it resists high oven temperature. Low-fat mozzarella can be used if you wish. To avoid overpowering the other ingredients with the mozzarella flavour, I recommend using very little mozzarella cheese

BASIL

This herb has made the Pizza Margherita very famous as it blends beautifully with tomatoes. There has, however, been much argument, especially in Naples, as to whether basil should be added to the pizza before or after it has been cooked. The old Neapolitans say basil should go in the oven with the rest of the ingredients to give all its fragrance and flavour to the pizza, but it's up to you if you would like to add it after cooking.

OVEN

The oven must be very hot to ensure the pizza cooks quickly, so preheat oven to the maximum heat, at least for 1 hour prior to cooking your pizza. Most pizzas take approximately 20 minutes to cook.

Position tray in oven: Fan-forced—any shelf
                            Electric—bottom of oven
                            Gas—middle shelf

A pizza stone can also be used in the oven to cook the pizza. The pizza stone will give a more authentic traditional tasting pizza. Taste will vary between pizza cooked in a tray and pizza cooked on a pizza stone.

When using a tray, always first brush the tray with oil before extending the dough, with your hands, on the tray.

BEN'S TIP: MY PERSONAL PREFERENCE IS TO PREPARE A MIXTURE OF OLIVE OIL AND CRUSHED GARLIC IN A BOWL AND LEAVE TO INFUSE. THEN, PRIOR TO PLACING PIZZA IN OVEN SPRINKLE THIS MIXTURE LIGHTLY ON TOP OF THE PIZZA TO GIVE EXTRA FLAVOUR TO THE BEAUTIFULLY COOKED PIZZA. OLIVE OIL ALONE CAN BE USED IF YOU PREFER.

WEIGHTS AND MEASURES

OVEN TEMPERATURES

100°C (200°F) = very slow = Gas Mark 1
120°C (250°F) = very slow = Gas Mark 1
140°C (275°F) = slow = Gas Mark 1
150°C (300°F) = slow = Gas Mark 2
160°C (325°F) = warm = Gas Mark 2–3
180°C (350°F) = moderate = Gas Mark 4
190°C (375°F) = moderately hot = Gas Mark 5
200°C (400°F) = hot = Gas Mark 6
220°C (420°F) = hot = Gas Mark 7
230°C (450°F) = very hot = Gas Mark 8
240°C (475°F) = very hot = Gas Mark 8–9
250°C (485°F) = very hot = Gas Mark 9
260°C (500°F)= very hot = Gas Mark 10

SOLID MEASURES

Metric and Imperial equivalents

10g = ¼oz
15g = ½oz
20g = ⅔oz
30g = 1oz
45g = 1½oz
60g = 2oz
90g = 3oz
100g = 3½ oz
125g = 4oz
150g = 5oz
165g = 5½ oz
180g = 6oz
200g = 6½ oz
220g = 7oz
250g = 8oz
300g = 10oz
350g = 11½ oz
400g = 13oz
500g = 1lb
750g = 1½lb
1kg = 2lb

FLUID MEASURES

Metric Imperial Standard cups

15ml = ⅔fl oz
20ml = 1fl oz
50ml = 1¾fl oz
60ml = 2fl oz
80ml = 2¾fl oz
100ml = 3½fl oz
125ml = 4fl oz
185ml = 6fl oz
200ml = 6½fl oz
250ml = 8fl oz
500ml = 16fl oz
750ml = 24fl oz
1L = 32fl oz

VEGETARIAN

PIZZA

MARGHERITA

MAKES A 30CM (12 INCH) DIAMETER PIZZA

INGREDIENTS

1 portion pizza dough (see 'The Basics of Pizza Making')
150g (5oz) crushed or peeled tomatoes, fresh or canned
1 teaspoon extra virgin olive oil
100g (3½oz) mozzarella shredded

METHOD

Preheat oven to highest temperature for 1 hour.
Oil a 30cm (12 inch) pizza tray. Using your fingers, spread the dough evenly over tray.
You can use a pizza stone if you have one.
Using a spoon, spread tomato on the dough, leaving a 1cm (½ inch) edge. Sprinkle
over shredded mozzarella.
Cook in oven for about 15–20 minutes.

CAPRESE

(TOMATO, BOCCONCINI AND BASIL)

MAKES A 30CM (12 INCH) DIAMETER PIZZA

INGREDIENTS

1 portion pizza dough (see 'The Basics of Pizza Making')
1 teaspoon extra virgin olive oil
200g (6½oz) crushed or peeled tomatoes, fresh or canned
100g (3½oz) bocconcini, sliced
Fresh basil leaves 4–5 leaves

METHOD

Preheat oven to highest temperature for 1 hour.
Oil a 30cm (12 inch) pizza tray. Using your fingers, spread the dough evenly over the
tray. You can use a pizza stone if you have one.
Using a spoon, spread tomato on the dough, leaving a 1cm ($^1/_2$ inch) edge. Layer
sliced bocconcini on top. Add basil leaves before or after cooking, according to taste.
Cook for about 15–20 minutes. Remove from oven and drizzle with olive oil
before serving.

BRUSCHETTA

MAKES A 30CM (12 INCH) DIAMETER PIZZA

INGREDIENTS

1 portion pizza dough (see 'The Basics of Pizza Making')
1 teaspoon olive oil
1 clove garlic, crushed
2 tomatoes, chopped
6 basil leaves, chopped
Salt

METHOD

Preheat oven to highest temperature for 1 hour.
Oil a 30cm (12 inch) pizza tray. Using your fingers, spread the dough evenly over tray.
You can use a pizza stone if you have one.
Using a fork, make small holes in the top of the pizza base.
In a small bowl, combine garlic and olive oil, and brush it over the pizza base. Cook
the pizza for about 15 minutes.
In a mixing bowl, combine the chopped tomatoes, crushed garlic, basil and olive oil.
Once mixed, add salt to taste. Set aside.
Remove from oven, top with tomato mixture and serve.

ST LUCIA

MAKES A 30CM (12 INCH) DIAMETER PIZZA

INGREDIENTS

1 portion pizza dough (see 'The Basics of Pizza Making')
1 teaspoon extra virgin olive oil
Pinch of rosemary
Salt to taste

METHOD

Preheat oven to highest temperature for 1 hour.

Oil a 30cm (12 inch) pizza tray or pizza stone. Using your fingers, spread the dough evenly over the pan.

Using a fork, make small holes on top of the pizza base.

Brush the extra virgin olive oil over the pizza, sprinkle with rosemary and add salt to taste.

Cook the pizza for about 10–15 minutes.

FUNGHI

(MUSHROOM)

MAKES A 30CM (12 INCH) DIAMETER PIZZA

INGREDIENTS

1 portion pizza dough (see 'The Basics of Pizza Making')
1 teaspoon olive oil
150g (5oz) crushed or peeled tomatoes, fresh or canned
100g (3½oz) mozzarella, shredded
100g (3½oz) mushrooms, sliced

METHOD

Preheat oven to highest temperature for 1 hour.
Oil a 30cm (12 inch) pizza tray. Using your fingers, spread the dough evenly over tray.
You can use a pizza stone if you have one.
Using a spoon, spread tomato on the dough leaving a 1cm (¹/₂ inch) edge.
Sprinkle over shredded mozzarella, then top with sliced mushrooms.
Cook for about 15–20 minutes.

MELANZANA

(EGGPLANT)

MAKES A 30CM (12 INCH) DIAMETER PIZZA

INGREDIENTS

1 portion pizza dough (see 'The Basics of Pizza Making')
1 teaspoon extra virgin olive oil
150g (5oz) crushed or peeled tomatoes, fresh or canned
2 tablespoons extra virgin olive oil, for frying
150g (5oz) eggplant, sliced
100g (3½oz) mozzarella shredded

METHOD

Preheat oven to highest temperature for 1 hour.
Oil a 30cm (12 inch) pizza tray. Using your fingers spread the dough evenly over tray.
You can use a pizza stone if you have one.
Using a spoon, spread tomato on the dough leaving a 1cm (¹/₂ inch) edge.
Heat oil in a pan and fry eggplant for approx 2 minutes, or alternatively grill on both
sides. Place eggplant slices on pizza. Sprinkle with shredded mozzarella.
Cook pizza for about 15–20 minutes.

VEGETARIANA

MAKES A 30CM (12 INCH) DIAMETER PIZZA

INGREDIENTS

1 portion pizza dough (see 'The Basics of Pizza Making')
1 teaspoon olive oil
150g (5oz) crushed or peeled tomatoes, fresh or canned
100g (3½oz) mozzarella, shredded
2 tablespoons olive oil, extra, for frying
70g (2½oz) green or red capsicum (bell peppers), sliced
100g (3½oz) eggplant, sliced
100g (3½oz) mushrooms, sliced
50g (1⅔oz) black olives, sliced
2 artichoke hearts, halved
1 onion, sliced

METHOD

Preheat oven to highest temperature for 1 hour.
Oil a 30cm (12 inch) pizza tray. Using your fingers, spread the dough evenly over tray.
You can use a pizza stone if you have one.
Using a spoon, spread tomato on the dough leaving a 1cm ($^1/_2$ inch) edge.
Sprinkle pizza with mozzarella.
Heat oil in a pan; fry the capsicum for 2 minutes. Fry or grill eggplant slices in olive
oil for approximately 2 minutes.
Top pizza with mushroom slices, capsicum, olives, eggplant, artichokes and onion.
Cook pizza for about 15-20 minutes.

AGLIO

(GARLIC)

MAKES A 30CM (12 INCH) DIAMETER PIZZA

INGREDIENTS

1 portion pizza dough (see 'The Basics of Pizza Making')
1 teaspoon olive oil
2 garlic cloves, crushed

METHOD

Preheat oven to highest temperature for 1 hour.
Oil a 30cm (12 inch) pizza tray. Using your fingers, spread the dough evenly over tray.
You can use a pizza stone if you have one.
Using a fork, make small holes in the top of the pizza base.
Mix garlic and olive oil, and brush it over the pizza base.
Cook the pizza for about 10–15 minutes.

BEN'S TIP: THIS MAKES A GREAT STARTER, USE IT INSTEAD OF GARLIC BREAD.

BUFFALA

(BUFFALO MOZZARELLA)

MAKES A 30CM (12 INCH) DIAMETER PIZZA

INGREDIENTS

1 portion pizza dough (see 'The Basics of Pizza Making')
1 teaspoon olive oil
200g (6½oz) buffala (buffalo) mozzarella
Six cherry tomatoes, halved
Five basil leaves

METHOD

Preheat oven to highest temperature for 1 hour.
Oil a 30cm (12 inch) pizza tray. Using your fingers, spread the dough
evenly over tray. You can use a pizza stone if you have one.
Break the mozzarella into pieces and place it around the pizza.
Place cherry tomato halves in between the buffalo mozzarella pieces, followed by the
basil and a drizzle of olive oil. (You can add basil after cooking if you prefer.)
Cook the pizza for about 15–20 minutes.

QUATTRO FORMAGGI

(FOUR CHEESES)

MAKES A 30CM (12 INCH) DIAMETER PIZZA

INGREDIENTS

1 portion pizza dough (see 'The Basics of Pizza Making')
2 tablespoons olive oil
150g (5oz) mozzarella, shredded
50g (1¾oz) gorgonzola, chopped
100g (3½oz) bocconcini, sliced
50g (1¾oz) parmesan, grated

METHOD

Preheat oven to highest temperature for 1 hour.
Oil a 30cm (12 inch) pizza tray. Using your fingers, spread the dough evenly over tray.
You can use a pizza stone if you have one.
Brush pizza with olive oil. Sprinkle mozzarella over pizza base, top with gorgonzola
and sliced boccincini. Finish with grated parmesan.
Cook the pizza for about 15–20 minutes.

AGLIO e MOZZARELLA

(GARLIC AND MOZZARELLA)

MAKES A 30CM (12 INCH) DIAMETER PIZZA

INGREDIENTS

1 portion pizza dough (see 'The Basics of Pizza Making')
1 teaspoon olive oil
1 garlic clove, crushed
100g (3½oz) mozzarella, shredded

METHOD

Preheat oven to highest temperature for 1 hour.
Oil a 30cm (12 inch) pizza tray. Using your fingers spread the dough evenly over the
tray. You can use a pizza stone if you have one.
Using a fork, make small holes on top of the pizza base.
Mix the crushed garlic with the olive oil and brush it over the pizza base, then
sprinkle over shredded mozzarella.
Cook the pizza for about 15 minutes.

CARCIOFI e FUNGHI

(ARTICHOKE AND MUSHROOM)

MAKES A 30CM (12 INCH) DIAMETER PIZZA

INGREDIENTS

1 portion pizza dough (see 'The Basics of Pizza Making')
1 teaspoon olive oil
4 artichoke hearts, halved
100g (3½oz) mushrooms, sliced
100g (3½oz) mozzarella, shredded

METHOD

Preheat oven to highest temperature for 1 hour.
Oil a 30cm (12 inch) pizza tray. Using your fingers, spread the dough evenly over the
tray. You can use a pizza stone if you have one.
Brush pizza with oil. Top with artichoke and mushrooms and
sprinkle with mozzarella.
Cook the pizza for about 15 minutes.

PATATA

(POTATO)

MAKES A 30CM (12 INCH) DIAMETER PIZZA

INGREDIENTS

1 portion pizza dough (see 'The Basics of Pizza Making')
1 teaspoon olive oil
150g (5oz) potatoes, boiled and sliced
1 onion, sliced
100g (3½oz) mozzarella, shredded
Sprig of rosemary
50g (1¾oz) parmesan cheese, grated
Salt to taste

METHOD

Preheat oven to highest temperature for 1 hour.
Oil a 30cm (12 inch) pizza tray. Using your fingers, spread the dough evenly over tray.
You can use a pizza stone if you have one.
Brush pizza with olive oil and top with sliced potatoes and onion. Sprinkle mozzarella
over the top, add rosemary and salt to taste, and finish with grated parmesan.
Cook pizza for about 15–20 minutes.

RICOTTA e SPINACI CALZONE

(RICOTTA AND SPINACH CALZONE)

MAKES A 30CM (12 INCH) DIAMETER PIZZA, FOLDED OVER

INGREDIENTS

1 portion pizza dough (see 'The Basics of Pizza Making)')
1 teaspoon olive oil
100g (3½oz) spinach
½ garlic clove, crushed, and mixed with olive oil
100g (3½oz) mozzarella, shredded
200g (7oz) ricotta
100g (3½oz) pizza sauce (see 'The Basics of Pizza' or use
bottled sauce)
20g (²⁄₃oz) parmesan, grated

METHOD

Preheat oven to highest temperature for 1 hour.
Oil a 30cm (12 inch) pizza tray. Using your fingers, spread the dough evenly over tray.
You can use a pizza stone if you have one.
In a frypan, cook spinach in garlic mixture for approx 2 minutes. Set aside to cool.
Sprinkle the shredded mozzarella on one half of the pizza, then top with ricotta, and
cooked spinach. Bring the other half of the pizza base over the ingredients.
Close the two sides with a fork or by pinching it around with your fingers.
Cook the calzone for about 15–20 minutes. Remove calzone from oven and pour over
sauce, sprinkle with parmesan and drizzle with olive oil.

SEAFOOD

PIZZA

GAMBERI

(PRAWNS)

MAKES A 30CM (12 INCH) DIAMETER PIZZA

INGREDIENTS

1 portion pizza dough (see 'The Basics of Pizza Making')

1 teaspoon extra virgin olive oil

150g (5oz) crushed or peeled tomatoes, fresh or canned

100g (3½oz) mozzarella, shredded

2 tablespoons olive oil, extra, for frying

9 medium sized green prawns, peeled

½ garlic clove, crushed

2 stems parsley, chopped

Salt to taste

METHOD

Preheat oven to highest temperature for 1 hour.

Oil a 30cm (12 inch) pizza tray. Using your fingers spread the dough evenly over tray.
You can use a pizza stone if you have one.

Using a spoon, spread tomato on the dough leaving a 1cm (1/2 inch) edge.

Sprinkle shredded mozzarella over pizza base.

Heat olive oil in a frypan and cook prawns with garlic and parsley, adding salt to
taste, for approximately 2 minutes.

Remove from pan and arrange prawns on top of pizza.

Cook for about 15–20 minutes.

COZZE

MAKES A 30CM (12 INCH) DIAMETER PIZZA

INGREDIENTS

1 portion pizza dough (see 'The Basics of Pizza Making')
1 teaspoon olive oil
150g (5oz) crushed or peeled tomatoes, fresh or canned
100g (3½oz) mozzarella shredded
1 dozen (100g or 3½oz) mussels in the shell
½ glass (125ml or 4fl oz) dry white wine
½ clove garlic, crushed

METHOD

Preheat oven to highest temperature for 1 hour.
Oil a 30cm (12 inch) pizza tray. Using your fingers, spread the dough evenly over tray.
You can use a pizza stone if you have one.
Using a spoon, spread tomato on the dough, leaving a 1cm (1/2 inch) edge.
Sprinkle mozzarella over tomato. In a pan, steam mussels in white wine for 2–5
minutes until they open, discarding any that remain closed.
Remove mussels from shells and place on top of pizza. Add garlic and olive oil
to taste. Cook the pizza for about 15–20 minutes.

TONNO e CIPOLLA

(TUNA AND ONION)

MAKES A 30CM (12 INCH) DIAMETER PIZZA

INGREDIENTS

1 portion pizza dough (see 'The Basics of Pizza Making')
1 teaspoon olive oil
100g (3½oz) mozzarella, shredded
1 x 250g (8oz) can tuna in oil
50g (1¾oz) onion, sliced

METHOD

Preheat oven to highest temperature for 1 hour.
Oil a 30cm (12 inch) pizza tray. Using your fingers, spread the dough evenly over tray.
You can use a pizza stone if you have one.
Brush pizza with oil. Top with mozzarella, tuna and sliced onion.
Cook the pizza for about 15–20 minutes.

FRUTTI DI MARE

(SEAFOOD)

MAKES A 30CM (12 INCH) DIAMETER PIZZA

INGREDIENTS

1 portion pizza dough (see 'The Basics of Pizza Making')

1 teaspoon olive oil

150g (5oz) crushed or peeled tomatoes, fresh or canned

100g (3½oz) mozzarella, shredded

6 mussels in the shell

12 baby clams in the shell

½ glass (125ml or 4fl oz) dry white wine

8 calamari rings

6 green prawns, peeled

½ garlic clove, crushed

2 stems parsley, chopped

Salt to taste

METHOD

Preheat oven to highest temperature for 1 hour. Oil a 30cm (12 inch) pizza tray. Using your fingers spread the dough evenly over tray. You can use a pizza stone if you have one. Using a spoon, spread tomato on the dough leaving a 1cm (¹/₂ inch) edge. Sprinkle over mozzarella.

In a pan, steam mussels and clams in white wine for 2–5 minutes until they open, discarding any that remain closed. Remove mussels and clams from shells and return to pan, add seafood and cook for 2 minutes. Add garlic, parsley and salt to taste. Top pizza with cooked seafood. Cook pizza for about 15–20 minutes.

MEAT

PIZZA

SCUGNIZZO

(STREET URCHIN)

MAKES A 30CM (12 INCH) DIAMETER PIZZA

INGREDIENTS

1 portion pizza dough (see 'The Basics of Pizza Making')
1 teaspoon extra virgin olive oil
150g (5oz) crushed or peeled tomatoes, fresh or canned
100g (3½oz) mozzarella, shredded
1 slice of shoulder ham, cut into 4 pieces
7 slices hot salami (Ventricina salami)

METHOD

Preheat oven to highest temperature for 1 hour.
Oil a 30cm (12 inch) pizza tray. Using your fingers, spread
the dough evenly over tray. You can use a pizza stone if you have one.
Using a spoon, spread tomato on the dough leaving a 1cm (1/2 inch) edge.
Sprinkle over shredded mozzarella, and then top with sliced ham. Place the salami
slices evenly over the pizza.
Cook for about 15–20 minutes.

BEN's TIP: I LIKE TO USE VENTRICINA SALAMI, WHICH IS AVAILABLE FROM
DELICATESSENS, BUT ANY HOT SALAMI WILL DO.

SALAMI

MAKES A 30CM (12 INCH) DIAMETER PIZZA

INGREDIENTS

1 portion pizza dough (see 'The Basics of Pizza Making')
1 teaspoon extra virgin olive oil
150g (5oz) crushed or peeled tomatoes, fresh or canned
100g (3½oz) mozzarella, shredded
7 slices salami

METHOD

Preheat oven to highest temperature for 1 hour.
Oil a 30cm (12 inch) pizza tray. Using your fingers spread the dough evenly over tray.
You can use a pizza stone if you have one.
Using a spoon, spread tomato on the dough leaving a 1cm (1/2 inch) edge.
Sprinkle over shredded mozzarella, then top with sliced salami.
Cook for about 15–20 minutes.

PROSCIUTTO COTTO

(HAM)

MAKES A 30CM (12 INCH) DIAMETER PIZZA

INGREDIENTS

1 portion pizza dough (see 'The Basics of Pizza Making')
1 teaspoon extra virgin olive oil
150g (5oz) crushed or peeled tomatoes, fresh or canned
100g (3½oz) mozzarella, shredded
2 slices of shoulder ham cut into quarters

METHOD

Preheat oven to highest temperature for 1 hour.
Oil a 30cm (12 inch) pizza tray. Using your fingers, spread the dough evenly over tray.
You can use a pizza stone if you have one.
Using a spoon, spread tomato on the dough leaving a 1cm (1/2 inch) edge.
Sprinkle over shredded mozzarella, and then top with sliced ham.
Cook for about 15–20 minutes.

CARNEVALE

MAKES A 30CM (12 INCH) DIAMETER PIZZA

INGREDIENTS

1 portion pizza dough (see 'The Basics of Pizza Making')
1 teaspoon olive oil
150g (5oz) crushed or peeled tomatoes, fresh or canned
100g (3½oz) mozzarella shredded
1 slice of shoulder ham cut into quarters
100g (3½oz) mushrooms, sliced
2 tablespoons olive oil, extra, for frying
70g (2⅓oz) green or red capsicum (bell pepper), sliced,
6 whole black olives
2 anchovy fillets in oil, cut into pieces

METHOD

Preheat oven to highest temperature for 1 hour.
Oil a 30cm (12 inch) pizza tray. Using your fingers, spread the dough evenly over tray.
You can use a pizza stone if you have one.
Using a spoon, spread tomato on the dough leaving a 1cm (1/2 inch) edge.
Sprinkle over mozzarella, add ham and mushrooms.
Heat olive oil in a pan and cooked capsicum for 2 minutes, remove from pan and
place on pizza. Add the whole black olives and anchovies.
Cook pizza for about 15–20 minutes.

CAPRICCIOSA

MAKES A 30CM (12 INCH) DIAMETER PIZZA

INGREDIENTS

1 portion pizza dough (see 'The Basics of Pizza Making')
1 teaspoon extra virgin olive oil
150g (5oz) crushed or peeled tomatoes, fresh or canned
100g (3½oz) mozzarella shredded
1 slice of shoulder ham, cut into quarters
100g (3½oz) mushrooms, sliced
6 whole black olives

METHOD

Preheat oven to highest temperature for 1 hour.
Oil a 30cm (12 inch) pizza tray. Using your fingers, spread the dough evenly over tray.
You can use a pizza stone if you have one.
Using a spoon, spread tomato on the dough leaving a 1cm (1/2 inch) edge.
Sprinkle over shredded mozzarella, and then top with ham, mushrooms
and whole black olives.
Cook for about 15–20 minutes.

QUATTRO STAGIONI

(FOUR SEASONS)

MAKES A 30CM (12 INCH) DIAMETER PIZZA

INGREDIENTS

1 portion pizza dough (see 'The Basics of Pizza Making')

1 teaspoon extra virgin olive oil

150g (5oz) crushed or peeled tomatoes, fresh or canned

100g (3½oz) mozzarella, shredded

100g (3½oz) mushrooms, sliced

6 whole black olives

1 hard-boiled egg, cut into quarters

4 slices prosciutto crudo

METHOD

Preheat oven to highest temperature for 1 hour. Oil a 30cm (12 inch) pizza tray. Using your fingers spread the dough evenly over tray. You can use a pizza stone if you have one. Using a spoon, spread tomato on the dough leaving a 1cm (1/2 inch) edge.
Sprinkle over mozzarella, add mushrooms and olives. Place hardboiled egg pieces on pizza. Cook pizza for about 15–20 minutes. Remove from oven, and top with sliced prosciutto before serving.

BEN'S TIP: PROSCIUTTO CRUDO LITERALLY MEANS 'RAW HAM'. THE HAM IS SEASONED, SALT-CURED AND AIR-DRIED SO IS READY TO EAT AS IS. IT IS AN ITALIAN DELICACY THAT IS READILY AVAILABLE IN SUPERMARKETS AND DELICATESSENS.

PICCANTE

(CHILLI)

MAKES A 30CM (12 INCH) DIAMETER PIZZA

INGREDIENTS

1 portion pizza dough (see 'The Basics of Pizza Making')
1 teaspoon extra virgin olive oil
150g (5oz) crushed or peeled tomatoes, fresh or canned
12 sundried tomatoes, sliced
100g (3½oz) hot cacciatore salami, sliced
1 small, red chilli, chopped finely
1 garlic clove, crushed and chopped

METHOD

Preheat oven to highest temperature for 1 hour.
Oil a 30cm (12 inch) pizza tray. Using your fingers spread the dough evenly over tray.
You can use a pizza stone if you have one.
Using a spoon, spread tomato on the dough leaving a 1cm (½ inch) edge.
Add sundried tomatoes, salami, chilli and garlic. Drizzle with olive oil and cook the
pizza for about 15–20 minutes.

SALSICCIA e SPINACI

(SAUSAGE AND SPINACH)

MAKES A 30CM (12 INCH) DIAMETER PIZZA

INGREDIENTS

1 portion pizza dough (see 'The Basics of Pizza Making')
1 teaspoon olive oil
150g (5oz) Italian sausage, sliced
100g (3½oz) spinach
1 garlic clove, crushed
100g (3½oz) mozzarella, shredded

METHOD

Preheat oven to highest temperature for 1 hour.
Oil a 30cm (12 inch) pizza tray. Using your fingers, spread the dough evenly over tray.
You can use a pizza stone if you have one.
Brush pizza with olive oil.
In a frypan, cook sausage, spinach and garlic and for approximately 2 minutes.
Remove from pan, place sausage slices on top of pizza. Top with spinach and garlic
and scatter with mozzarella.
Cook the pizza for about 15–20 minutes.

SALSICCIA e CIPOLLA

(SAUSAGE AND ONION)

MAKES A 30CM (12 INCH) DIAMETER PIZZA.

INGREDIENTS

1 portion pizza dough (see 'The Basics of Pizza Making')
1 teaspoon olive oil
1 onion, sliced
150g (5oz) Italian sausage, sliced
100g (3½oz) mozzarella, shredded

METHOD

Preheat oven to highest temperature for 1 hour.
Oil a 30cm (12 inch) pizza tray. Using your fingers, spread the dough evenly over tray.
You can use a pizza stone if you have one.
Brush pizza with a little olive oil.
Heat olive oil in a pan, add onion slices and sausage and cook for approx 2 minutes.
Remove from pan, arrange on top of pizza and scatter with mozzarella.
Cook the pizza for about 15–20 minutes.

TROPICALE

MAKES A 30CM (12 INCH) DIAMETER PIZZA

INGREDIENTS

1 portion pizza dough (see 'The Basics of Pizza Making')
1 teaspoon olive oil
150g (5oz) crushed or peeled tomatoes, fresh or canned
100g (3½oz) mozzarella shredded
2 slices shoulder ham cut into quarters
100g (3½oz) pineapples pieces

METHOD

Preheat oven to highest temperature for 1 hour.
Oil a 30cm (12 inch) pizza tray. Using your fingers spread the dough evenly over tray.
You can use a pizza stone if you have one.
Using a spoon, spread tomato on the dough leaving a 1cm (1/2 inch) edge.
Sprinkle over mozzarella, and then top with ham quarters and pineapple pieces.
Cook pizza for about 15–20 minutes.

RUCOLA e PROSCIUTTO CRUDO

(ROCKET AND PROSCIUTTO)

MAKES A 30CM (12 INCH) DIAMETER PIZZA

INGREDIENTS

1 portion pizza dough (see 'The Basics of Pizza Making')
1 teaspoon extra virgin olive oil
150g (5oz) crushed or peeled tomatoes, fresh or canned
100g (3½oz) mozzarella, shredded
1 bunch of rocket leaves
50g (1²⁄₃oz) parmesan cheese, shaved or grated
4 slices of prosciutto crudo

METHOD

Preheat oven to highest temperature for 1 hour.
Oil a 30cm (12 inch) pizza tray. Using your fingers spread the dough evenly over tray.
You can use a pizza stone if you have one.
Using a spoon, spread tomato on the dough leaving a 1cm (1/2 inch) edge.
Sprinkle over mozzarella.
Cook the pizza for about 15–20 minutes. Remove from oven, and top with rocket and parmesan. Drizzle with olive oil and top with sliced prosciutto before serving.

SALAMI CALZONE

MAKES A 30CM (12 INCH) DIAMETER PIZZA FOLDED IN HALF

INGREDIENTS

I portion pizza dough (see 'The Basics of Pizza Making')

I teaspoon olive oil

100g (3½oz) mozzarella shredded

7 slices hot salami (Ventricina salami)

100g (3½oz) mushrooms, sliced

50g (1¾oz) black olives, sliced

I clove garlic, crushed and mixed with olive oil

100g (3½oz) pizza sauce (see 'The Basics of Pizza Making'), or
use bottled sauce

20g (⅔oz) parmesan cheese, grated

METHOD

Preheat oven to highest temperature for 1 hour.

Oil a 30cm (12 inch) pizza tray. Using your fingers, spread the dough evenly over tray.
You can use a pizza stone if you have one.

Top one half of the pizza with mozzarella, salami, mushrooms and olives.

Add the garlic and oil mixture; fold the other half of the base over the ingredients.

Close the two sides with a fork or by pinching it around with your fingers.

Cook the calzone for about 15–20 minutes. Remove calzone from the oven and pour
pizza sauce over. Sprinkle with parmesan cheese and a drizzle of olive oil.

RICOTTA e PROSCIUTTO COTTO CALZONE

(RICOTTA AND HAM CALZONE)

MAKES A 30CM (12 INCH) DIAMETER PIZZA, FOLDED IN HALF

INGREDIENTS

1 portion pizza dough (see 'The Basics of Pizza Making')
1 teaspoon olive oil
100g (3½oz) mozzarella, shredded
250g (8oz) ricotta
1 slice of shoulder ham, cut into quarters
100g (3½oz) pizza sauce (see 'The Basics of Pizza Making'), or
use bottled sauce
20g (¾oz) parmesan, grated

METHOD

Preheat oven to highest temperature for 1 hour.
Oil a 30cm (12 inch) pizza tray. Using your fingers, spread the dough evenly over pan.
You can use a pizza stone if you have one.
Top one half of the pizza with mozzarella, ricotta and ham. Bring the other half of the
pizza base over the ingredients.
Close the two sides with a fork or by pinching it around with your fingers.
Cook the calzone for about 15–20 minutes. Remove calzone from oven, pour sauce
over, sprinkle with grated parmesan cheese and drizzle with olive oil.

CALZONE FRITTO

(FRIED CALZONE)

MAKES A 30CM (12 INCH) DIAMETER PIZZA FOLDED IN HALF

INGREDIENTS

1 portion pizza dough (see 'The Basics of Pizza Making')
1 teaspoon olive oil
2 cups olive oil, extra for frying.
100g (3½oz) mozzarella, shredded
10 slices cacciatore salami
200g (7oz) ricotta

METHOD

Oil a 30cm (12 inch) pizza tray. Using your fingers, spread the dough evenly over tray.
Sprinkle mozzarella on one half of the pizza, then top with ricotta and salami.
Fold the other half of the pizza base over the ingredients. Close the two sides with a
fork or by pinching it around with your fingers.
Fill a deep frying pan with oil and bring to the boil. Cook calzone in oil until golden
brown on both sides, turning regularly. Serve immediately.

BEN'S TIP: USE ANY TYPE OF SALAMI IF CACCIATORE IS NOT AVAILABLE.

SPECIALITIES OF THE HOUSE

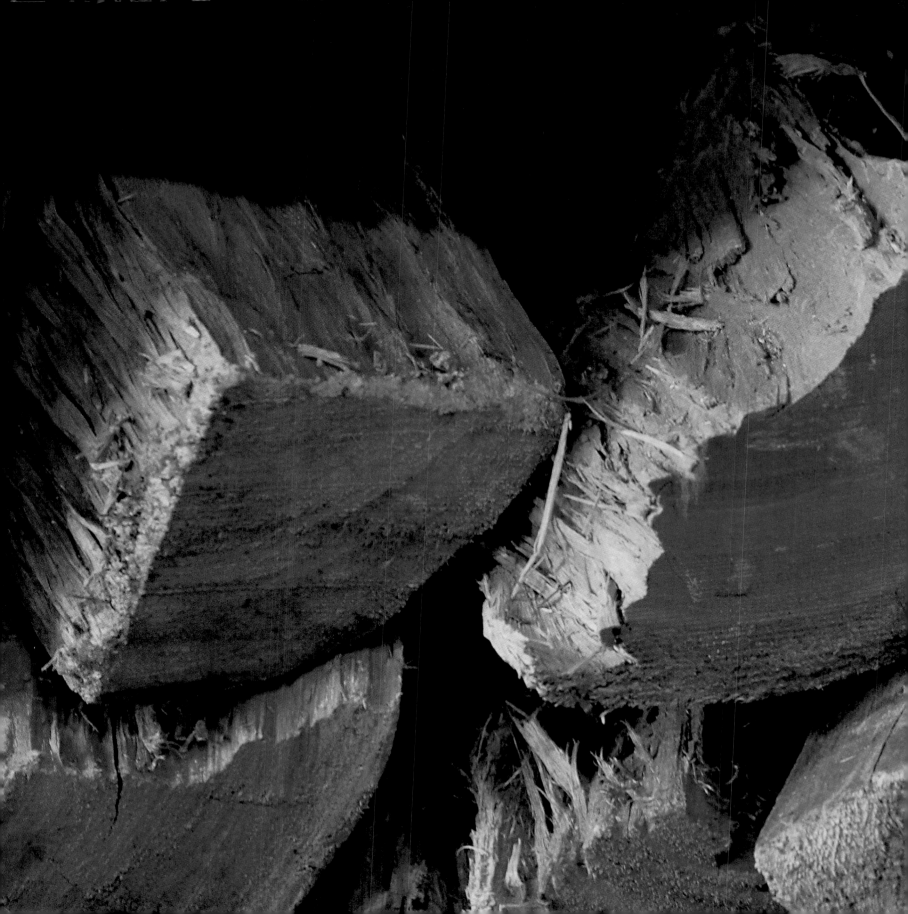

FRITTELLE DI NANNATA

(WHITEBAIT)

Serves 4 as an entree

INGREDIENTS

1 cup unbleached or plain flour
4 eggs, lightly beaten
Salt to taste
½ clove garlic, crushed
2 stems parsley, chopped
100g (3½oz) parmesan cheese, grated
500g (1lb) whitebait
2 cups olive oil, for frying

METHOD

Place flour, eggs, salt, crushed garlic, chopped parsley, grated parmesan cheese
and whitebait into a mixing bowl and combine with a spoon until the mixture has a
smooth texture, and is neither too thick or runny.
Heat the olive oil in a frying pan until hot. With a spoon, scoop white bait mixture
into patty shapes and deep fry until golden on both sides.
Remove patties from oil and place on paper towels to remove excess oil.

MARINARA

(THE ORIGINAL SAILOR'S PIZZA)

MAKES A 30CM (12 INCH) DIAMETER PIZZA

INGREDIENTS

1 portion pizza dough (see 'The Basics of Pizza Making')
1 teaspoon extra virgin olive oil
150g (5oz) fresh tomatoes, or
1 x 410g (13oz) can tinned crushed tomatoes
1 garlic clove, chopped
1 teaspoob oregano
Salt to taste

METHOD

Preheat oven to highest temperature for 1 hour.
Oil a 30cm (12 inch) pizza tray. Using your fingers spread the dough
evenly over tray. You can use a pizza stone if you have one.
Using a spoon, spread tomato on the dough leaving a 1cm (1/2 inch) edge. Sprinkle
over garlic and oregano, and drizzle with oil. Add salt to taste.
Cook pizza for about 15–20 minutes.

NAPOLI

IN

BOCCA

RISTORAN

CALAMARI RIPIENI

(STUFFED CALAMARI)

Serves 4 as an entree

INGREDIENTS

6 calamari tubes, cleaned
400g (13oz) green prawns, peeled
200g (6½oz) clam meat
½ cup olive oil
2 stems parsley, chopped
1 clove garlic, crushed
Salt to taste
50g (1¾oz) breadcrumbs
300g (10½oz) Napoletana sauce (see 'The Basics of Pizza
Making') or use bottled sauce
½ glass (125ml/4fl oz) dry white wine

METHOD

Chop two calamari tubes, prawns and clam meat into small pieces. Heat oil in a fry pan, add seafood mixture, parsley, garlic and salt. Fry for approximately 5 minutes. Add the breadcrumbs to the frypan and mix thoroughly. Allow mixture to cool. Using a spoon, fill remaining calamari tubes with fish and crumb mixture until they are ¾ full. Close top of calamari tubes by weaving a toothpick through the top. Place closed calamari inside a flameproof dish, pour over white wine and Napoletana sauce to cover and simmer for approx 10–15 minutes, turning tubes regularly.

FIORI DI ZUCCHINE

(STUFFED ZUCCHINI FLOWERS)

SERVES 4 AS AN ENTREE

INGREDIENTS

100g (3½oz) mozzarella, shredded
6 anchovy fillets in oil, chopped
20 zucchini flowers
250g (8oz) plain flour
250ml (8oz) sparkling mineral water
Salt to taste
2 cups olive oil, for frying

METHOD

In a mixing bowl, combine mozzarella and anchovies.
Using a spoon, carefully remove pulp from zucchini flowers, then fill each flower with
mozzarella and anchovy mix and set aside.
In a mixing bowl, combine flour, mineral water and salt, mixing until all ingredients
are thoroughly combined.
Coat stuffed zucchini flowers with batter. Heat olive oil in a fry pan and fry battered
zucchini flowers until golden brown. Remove from oil and place on paper towel to
drain excess oil.

PANZEROTTI

MAKES 4

INGREDIENTS

1 portion pizza dough (see 'The Basics of Pizza Making')
100g (3½oz) mozzarella, shredded
8 cherry tomatoes, chopped
2 cups olive oil, for frying

METHOD

Divide the pizza dough in quarters and stretch out to make 4 small round pizzette.
Sprinkle shredded mozzarella on one half of each pizzette and top with
cherry tomatoes.
Fold the other half of the pizza base over the ingredients. Close the two sides with
a fork or by pinching it around with your fingers.
Heat oil in a frying pan with oil. Bring to boil and cook panzerotti in the oil until
golden brown on both sides, turning frequently.
Serve immediately.

PIZZA FIORI DI ZUCCHINI

(ZUCCHINI FLOWER PIZZA)

MAKES A 30CM (12 INCH) DIAMETER PIZZA

INGREDIENTS

1 portion pizza dough (see 'The Basics of Pizza Making')
1 teaspoon olive oil
100g (3½oz) mozzarella, shredded
6 anchovy fillets in oil, chopped
15 zucchini flowers
1 tablespoon breadcrumbs
Salt to taste
Black peppercorns

METHOD

Preheat oven to highest temperature for 1 hour.
Oil a 30cm (12 inch) pizza tray. Using your fingers, spread the dough evenly over tray.
You can use a pizza stone if you have one.
Add mozzarella, zucchini flowers and anchovies. Sprinkle breadcrumbs over the top,
season to taste with salt and pepper and drizzle with olive oil.
Cook the pizza for about 15–20 minutes.

COZZE SUGO PICCANTE

(MUSSELS IN SPICY TOMATO SAUCE)

Serves 1

INGREDIENTS

20 mussels in the shell

1 glass (250ml/8fl oz) dry white wine

3 tablespoons olive oil

1 garlic clove, crushed

Pinch chilli flakes

Salt to taste

2 stems parsley, chopped

600ml (21¼fl oz) Napoletana sauce (see 'The Basics of Pizza'

or use bottled variety)

METHOD

Place mussels into a flameproof casserole dish, pour wine over and cover with lid.
Reduce heat and steam mussels for two minutes, or until mussel shells are opened.
Discard any that do not open.
Add olive oil, crushed garlic, chilli flakes, salt and chopped parsley and simmer for
a further two minutes.
Pour in Napoletana sauce and simmer for approximately five minutes.
Pour mussel soup into a deep bowl and sprinkle with chopped parsley to serve.

SPAGHETTI VONGOLE

(CLAM SPAGHETTI)

Serves 4

INGREDIENTS

200g (8oz) vongole (baby clams), in the shell
½ glass (125ml/4fl oz) dry white wine
3 tablespoons olive oil
½ clove garlic, crushed
10 cherry tomatoes, halved
500g (1lb) spaghetti
2 parsley stems, chopped
Salt to taste

METHOD

Heat a frypan and add vognole, pour over wine and steam with lid on until all shells open up, discarding any vongole that remain closed. Add olive oil, garlic and tomatoes and simmer for approximately 2 minutes.
Meanwhile, fill a pot three-quarters full with water and bring to boil. Add the spaghetti and cook it al dente, or according to packet directions.
Once cooked, drain pasta and toss in pan with clam mixture, adding parsley and salt to taste, until well combined.

VESUVIANA

Makes a 30cm (12 inch) diameter pizza.

INGREDIENTS

1 portion pizza dough (see 'The Basics of Pizza Making')
1 teaspoon olive oil
150g (5oz) crushed or peeled tomatoes, fresh or canned
100g (3½oz) mozzarella, shredded
12 whole black olives
6 anchovy fillets in oil, drained and chopped
Pinch of oregano

METHOD

Preheat oven to highest temperature for 1 hour.
Oil a 30cm (12 inch) pizza tray. Using your fingers spread the dough evenly over tray.
You can use a pizza stone if you have one.
Using a spoon, spread tomato on the dough leaving a 1cm (½inch) edge.
Sprinkle with shredded mozzarella, then top with whole olives and anchovy. Sprinkle
with oregano.
Cook for about 15–20 minutes.

LINGUINE CON POLLO e PESTO

(CHICKEN AND PESTO LINGUINE)

Serves 4

INGREDIENTS

300g (10oz) chicken fillets
¼ cup plain flour
2 tablespoons olive oil
100ml (3½fl oz) pre-prepared pesto
250ml (8fl oz) fresh cream
Salt to taste
500g (1lb) linguine
100g (3½oz) parmesan cheese, grated

METHOD

Dust chicken fillets in flour. Heat oil in a pan and fry chicken until cooked. Remove from pan and allow to cool before slicing into small pieces.
Return chicken pieces to frypan and add pesto and cream, and heat until simmering for approximately 5 minutes.
Fill a large saucepan three-quarters full with water and bring to the boil. Add linguine and cook it al dente, or according to packet directions.
Drain cooked pasta and toss in frypan with other ingredients until well mixed. Add salt to taste and serve sprinkled with parmesan.

GNOCCHI ROSA

SERVES 1–2

INGREDIENTS

300g (10oz) gnocchi (potato dumplings)
300g (10oz) Napoletana sauce (see 'The Basics of Pizza
Making') or use bottled sauce
50ml (1²⁄₃oz) fresh cream
100g (3½oz) grated parmesan cheese

METHOD

Fill a large saucepan three-quarters full with water, add salt and bring to boil. Add gnocchi and cook, removing them from the saucepan with a slotted spoon when they rise to the surface.

Meanwhile, heat Napoletana sauce and cream in a frypan and simmer for approximately 2–3 minutes.

Add cooked gnocchi to simmering sauce, add parmesan and salt to taste and combine until well mixed. Cook for a further 5 minutes until sauce thickens.

RISOTTO NAPOLI

SERVES 2

INGREDIENTS

60g (2oz) plain flour
100g (3½oz) chicken fillets
4 tablespoons olive oil
½ clove garlic, crushed
100g (3½oz) mushrooms, sliced
300g (10oz) arborio rice
50ml (1⅔oz) fresh cream
300g (10oz) Napoletana sauce (see 'The Basics of Pizza
Making') or use bottled sauce
100g (3½oz) parmesan, grated
Salt to taste

METHOD

Dust chicken with flour. Heat half the olive oil in a pan and fry chicken until cooked.
Remove from pan and allow to cool before slicing into small pieces.
Return fry pan to heat, add remaining olive oil and garlic, mushrooms and cooked
chicken and simmer for approximately 2 minutes.
Fill a large saucepan three quarters full with water, add salt and bring to the boil. Add
rice and cook till al dente. Once cooked drain rice into a colander. Add rice to frypan
with chicken mixture, add Napoletana sauce, cream, grated parmesan and salt to
taste, and combine well.

SPAGHETTI CON POLPETTE

(SPAGHETTI WITH MEATBALLS)

SERVES 4

INGREDIENTS

200g (6½oz) beef mince

2 stems parsley, chopped

1 clove garlic, crushed

50g (1²/₃oz) parmesan, grated

1 egg, lightly beaten

20g (²/₃oz) breadcrumbs

Salt to taste

2 cups olive oil

500g (1lb) spaghetti

600ml (21fl oz) Napoletana sauce (see 'The Basics of Pizza making') or use bottled sauce

METHOD

In a large bowl combine mince, parsley, garlic, parmesan, egg, breadcrumbs and salt to taste. Using a spoon, mix all the ingredients together. Scoop the mixture and roll into small balls. Heat olive oil in a pan and fry the meatballs until golden brown. Remove meatballs from pan and place on paper towels to drain excess oil.

Fill a large saucepan three-quarters full with water and bring to the boil. Add spaghetti and cook till al dente, or according to packet instructions.

Meanwhile, return pan to heat, add sauce and meatballs and simmer for approximately 5 minutes.

Drain cooked pasta into a colander and add to the pan with meatballs and toss until well combined.

MOZZARELLA IN CARROZZA

(MOZZARELLA PARCELS)

SERVES 4

INGREDIENTS

8 slices white sliced bread

200g (6½oz) mozzarella, shredded

250g (8oz) plain flour

4 eggs

4 tablespoons milk

Salt to taste

2 cups oil for frying

METHOD

Cut the crusts off the bread slices.

Divide mozzarella cheese between 4 slices of bread, and top with remaining bread, making 4 sandwiches or pizzettes.

Place plain flour on a plate. In a small bowl, whisk eggs, milk and salt until combined.

Dust sandwiches with flour, and coat both sides in egg mixture.

Fill a deep pan with oil. Heat oil to boiling and cook pizzettes until both sides are golden brown, turning regularly.

Once cooked, remove from oil and place on paper towels to drain excess oil.

Serve while still warm.

VECCHIA NAPOLI

Makes a 30cm (12 inch) diameter pizza

INGREDIENTS

1 portion pizza dough (see 'The Basics of Pizza Making')
1 teaspoon olive oil
150g (5oz) crushed or peeled tomatoes, fresh or canned
100g (3½oz) mozzarella shredded
40g (1½oz) capers
6 anchovy fillets in oil, chopped
Pinch of oregano

METHOD

Preheat oven to highest temperature for 1 hour.
Oil a 30cm (12 inch) pizza tray. Using your fingers spread the dough evenly over tray.
You can use a pizza stone if you have one.
Using a spoon, spread tomato on the dough leaving a 1cm (½ inch) edge.
Sprinkle with mozzarella, add capers then anchovies. Sprinkle with oregano. Cook the
pizza for about 15–20 minutes.

SWEET

PIZZA

PIZZA NUTELLA

Makes a 30cm (12 inch) diameter pizza

INGREDIENTS

1 portion pizza dough (see 'The Basics of Pizza Making')
100g (3½oz) Nutella or other hazelnut spread
10 strawberries, halved
1 teaspoon icing sugar to sprinkle

METHOD

Preheat oven to highest temperature for one hour.
Using your fingers, spread the dough evenly over a 30cm (12 inch) tray. You can use a
pizza stone if you have one.
Cook the pizza for about 10 minutes.
Remove from oven and, with a spoon, spread nutella or hazelnut spread all over the
pizza. Top with strawberries and sprinkle icing sugar.

RICOTTA e FRUTTA

(RICOTTA AND FRUIT)

Makes a 30cm (12 inch) diameter pizza

INGREDIENTS

1 portion pizza dough (see 'The Basics of Pizza Making')
250g (8oz) fresh ricotta
6 teaspoons cocoa powder
½ glass (125ml/4fl oz) milk
1 orange, peeled and cut into segments
1 lemon, peeled and cut into segments
1 green pear, cut into thin slices
1 punnet strawberries, hulls removed and halved
2 pineapple rings, diced

METHOD

Preheat oven to highest temperature for one hour. Using your fingers, spread the
dough evenly over a 30cm (12 inch) pizza tray. You can use a pizza stone if you have
one. Using a knife, spread fresh ricotta over the pizza.
Cook the pizza for about 15 minutes.
Meanwhile, in a saucepan warm milk and blend in cocoa powder
to form a thick syrup.
Once pizza is cooked, top with fruit and return to oven for a further 5 minutes.
Remove from oven and pour warm chocolate syrup over pizza before serving.

PIZZA CON LE FRAGOLE e CREMA

(STRAWBERRIES AND CREAM PIZZA)

MAKES A 30CM (12 INCH) DIAMETER PIZZA

INGREDIENTS

1 portion pizza dough (see 'The Basics of Pizza Making')
300g (10½oz) custard cream
250g (8oz) can whipped cream
1 punnet strawberries, halved
1 teaspoon icing sugar to dust

METHOD

Preheat oven to highest temperature for one hour.
Using your fingers, spread the dough evenly over a 30cm (12 inch) tray. You can use a
pizza stone if you have one.
Using a knife, spread the custard cream over the pizza.
Cook the pizza for about 20–25 minutes.
Remove from the oven, decorate with balls of whipped cream around the edge of the
pizza, add strawberry halves and dust with icing sugar.

ABOUT THE AUTHOR

I was born just outside Naples and moved to Australia with my family at the age of 13. Growing up, I had a passion for pizza as I watched my mother and grandmother preparing them at home. We maintained this tradition when we moved. Even as a teenager I would make pizza for my friends and relatives.

I loved pizza so much that in 1977, after managing a number of restaurants, hotels and clubs, I opened my first restaurant in Sydney, which was an existing restaurant operated by a fellow Neapolitan. It was here that I learned the electric pizza oven was not able to produce the traditional Pizza Napoletana that I wanted, and was making at home. The traditional Pizza Napoletana is at its best when produced in a wood-fired oven.

My passion for pizza was so strong that I had a wood-fired oven built at my home in Haberfield in Sydney, and made pizza for friends, relatives and the neighbors who were attracted by the aromas wafting from my back yard.

In 1995 I was employed as a hotel restaurant manager, and I decided to open a pizza restaurant close to my Haberfield home. To ensure we produced the traditional Pizza Napoletana, I installed an authentic wood-fired pizza oven imported from Italy.

The restaurant started as a hobby to indulge my passion for pizza and—contrary to the skeptics who didn't believe that a traditional pizza restaurant could succeed in this quiet family suburb—we are still here. *Napoli In Bocca* (Naples in Your Mouth) was born and the local Italian community became regulars as they enjoyed the traditional pizza, sitting for hours at the tables reminiscing of the pizza in their villages in Italy.

INDEX

First published in Australia in 2010 by
New Holland Publishers (Australia) Pty Ltd
Sydney • Auckland • London • Cape Town

1/66 Gibbes Street Chatswood NSW 2067 Australia
218 Lake Road Northcote Auckland New Zealand
86 Edgware Road London W2 2EA United Kingdom
80 McKenzie Street Cape Town 8001 South Africa

National Library of Australia Cataloguing-in-Publication entry
Riccio, Ben.
Pizza from Naples / Ben Riccio.
1st ed.
9781741108859 (pbk.)
Pizza.
Cookery.
641.8248

Publisher: Diane Jardine
Publishing Manager: Lliane Clarke
Editor: Rochelle Fernandez
Designer: Emma Gough
Photographs: Graeme Gillies
Production Manager: Olga Dementiev
Printer: Toppan Leefung Printing Limited

10 9 8 7 6 5 4 3 2